I0423935

Dedication

This book is dedicated to the elimination of the worse kind of party pooper that has ever existed.

This can help people choose qualified leaders
And help those we choose become better leaders

Dismiss the Fear Factors in America in Order to:

1. Stop Spiritual Wars
2. Stop Towerism in America
3. Prevent a possible terrorist attack
4. Learn spiritual skills

Welcome to the Coming Out of the Sublime
It is a wonderful thing!

This book is like taking steps up to freedom to climb out of an old stale atmosphere

We are now gearing up to be a silent majority. The enemy won't know we are there until we have succeeded in getting on point across or we have won the process in growth the right way, without violence.

This is one of the best views on earth
That provides invaluable insight

The Power of The Lord's Persuasion

It Can be revealed when you keep saying (over and over), "Satan fly pass me; Satan die pass me!"

Then say to the Lord, "Please don't pass me by!"

It may have only taken one man to start this but it is going to take many men to complete it.

This may be considered a short book but it can take a big bite out of crime to help stop it in our lifetime.

This can be looked at as a spiritual renewal project that gives a way to develop the process of using spiritual skills as was done back in history.

PEOPLE WANTED!

The first audience is in heaven;

The second is on earth,

who is your biggest audience?

This Book is on God's best seller's list

A Note to Philly

Taking notice that it appears that the Democratic Party doesn't have a problem like the Republican Party does and that there is no kind of violence that may be looming on the horizon, we can say what may be a different kind of process still has an element of danger that may or can come to the city as any other cities in the countries. The thing we are taking a close look at is the threat of a possible terrorist attack.

Therefore, the City of Philadelphia can also benefit from the use of the material that helps to provide added protection on many levels of conscious awareness. This can keep the people on their toes, lift their spirits and give them a coat of armor they can be proud to wear.

Join in to keep winning in life!

Don't Deny the Power of Agape Love

Now, what a great day to have a star-clism
This word represents a new cluster of stars.

Singe This Into Your Spirit!

It is time to stop walking sightless
among miracles that can be made to appear!

In an Upcoming Book, the Power of Knowing "No"
is coming to your life sooner that you expect

I have no sorrows from Knowing "No"

Acknowledging as far as the eyes can see the principals of this methodology will work for one person or a multitude of people; the more the merrier.

People must be doing something mighty powerful for the devil to pass them by.

It is time to stop or get rid of the invisible crutches and walk like a cripple because you don't really need them.

The messages being brought forth are preventive. They are based on level of spiritual faith health.

Now who will step forward to lead the charge?

The next step is to get the word out to make
it be known to all!

A Plan for the City

Test the water read the book and judge for yourself to help you make up your mind to help or not. Now think, how many problems do we have that are put together for one issue that we can avoid and repair? It is up to us.

I am a messenger and a shepherd also

Here comes a presence of thought that may take a little time to focus on being human we face things that sometimes are hard to grasp but with this, try.

We can prevent a spiritual warfare from landing on earth. There comes a time when we do not have only commercial tools to fix something when it is broken to stop it from getting even worse like a dam breaking loose.

If an unwise person predicts a major problem is going to happen in the city of Cleveland, we as godly people can stop the process, with the truth about the counterfeit way it came about in the first place. Donald Trump said there will be a riot if he is not nominated. Now at a time when there is apprehension and tension, it seems quite devilish to make comments like that.

Who is it that predicted it? A troubled man. What does this man have that got him where he is at? Being somewhat business savvy with a degree of success. Saying all this I feel this person has a personal problem; it is called towerism. Is this new? No. Can it be fixed? Yes but not in time, with this person personally, before the voting process stops. Therefore, we have to fix the atmosphere, by removing the wick from the wicked that some people have in them to show them how to not go to the powder keg.

Now if you don't want to dump the trump just dump the dumb part of the man that has an "ism" to be known as towerism. Thank you.

This is referencing the prediction of a riot. I claim it not to happen in the name of the Lord because there will be peace in the village of Cleveland, Ohio. We will not let Satan take and create a stronghold on the city that creates some kind of hell hole from the madness. Thanks to the power that is within the people who believe in justice and know Satan, we will see the accomplishments of Cleveland not destroyed or set back. Now Satan wants to stop progress and destroy what it took a lifetime for some to see, the now goodness of what was once known as the mistake by the lake. Now it is becoming beautiful as it was meant to be and one of the greatest locations in the nation.

Therefore, I implore you to raise your arms to give thanks that no weapons formed against the city of Cleveland, Ohio shall prosper. Make it known that we are a blessed town and shall stay blessed until the end of this life we know and another one better comes along.

Now can we complete the work on our side at Bound to Heaven Publishing/Ministries? Yes because long before the city knew of getting the RNC coming here the Lord knew. That is why he had this plan put together to help prevent harm if need be to the city and people. This plan also helped stop the outbreak of trouble when some folks wanted to get out of line this past year because of injustices.

Don't discount whatever level of peace that adds love to the presence of the negativity that others may want to bring with a process of evil that may help stop it. I hope we can see the solution to any problem that wants to create an uprising on a bad state of affairs.

To The Public at Large

I am sending out a request to all people of adult age. If you live in the city of Cleveland or surrounding counties, we are in need of the extra eyes and ears to test your perception to a level of what could be newness.

We are looking for volunteers to try a new kind of insight that may give you the ability to detect a foreign invader that may have intention to do harm to the city and the people within it.

Now this can be a position of paid that will only give you an opportunity to learn a new level of living with what could be incredible insight to the future in a positive way. It could create a way to have a vision that will open up a door to greatness in a way of prevention and detection that makes the love you have for mankind greater than ever. Besides, the city and its people need not see destruction that can set back progress.

If preventative measures can be put in place to help save millions of dollars, create jobs and keep improving city services; that is better for the community. Therefore if you feel a need to help keep Cleveland growing, thriving and healthy, let's do this for ourselves, individually as well as the body of Christ.

To Clear Things Up; What are the Benefits?

1. Help prevent mayhem and rioting;
2. Give people hope that they are safe in our cities;
3. Show the world that we have a loving atmosphere;
4. Help develop a new level of growth in our country and its people.

Now, I say amen and hallelujah because of the best part of it; it creates a place of peace where the Lord doesn't let confusion in. Getting it from the messenger's mouth – there's no hotter ticket in the country to be had.

The time has come to know we are able
to stop this kind of manmade disaster!

Funding is needed to increase the product line of books that can help with the prevention of an enemy that may have plans to attack the USA and at the time of the conventions in Cleveland, Ohio and Philadelphia, PA.

If we are helping to prevent trouble from problems between the police and people, can we also help prevent what could be a bigger problem at the RNC that is coming to Cleveland? I think so and we have a way to help get it done!

1. Stopping a spiritual warfare that can open us up to more of the work Satan wants to do to hurt people and it is not about America, it is about he gets in where he can.

2. Exposing towerists to start ending towerism by defining a new sickness even if it is a spiritual kind and fix it.

3. Make the people know of this to read between the lines themselves in closing.

4. Start to rid the country of bad politicians. This can also help save a part of the world.

This is the helium that fills the balloons of healing so they can rise.

This Can be a Proposal to Anyone

Now to the people in charge of the safety of the city of Cleveland, Ohio: if you have been given $50 million, you would be better off putting some of the money in this way of prevention than wasting it in a lot of other ways. Don't you think so?

Oh ye of little faith, the Lord said I will not leave nor forsake you. Now, how ridiculous it is that some believe in a process that creates fear and the government of the country even believes in a process that creates fear so much just to supposedly do the right thing, they set aside $50 million to protect it. How ridiculous is this? You answer that!

We have the time to show people a way around the worldliness that reflects bad things happening that can harm others. God's love is in the process of defeating the enemy that is within some of the people in the world, even if they don't know it is there or believe it is not there. This can be done without harming anyone with the truth to set them free and bring joy to their soul, in order for them to know of the gospel of how the love of the Lord can work things out and create a way out of what appears to be no way.

Therefore, it is time to not show up to show out but to show up and give praise and thanks for life everlasting because we shall overcome and the victory can be shared. Now in order for us to know this in our hearts we must learn it for ourselves then teach it to others.

At the free stamp in downtown Cleveland as a part of the winning team with the B-ball game. I talk about the winner in the books before it came to pass. The people are not complaining about the fact the city being known as a city with a curse. Now how will they feel about the new blessing.

Additional learning material on this and similar topics is at Amazon.com in a book titled _Ending Spiritual Warfare in America_. Get a copy please to help stop what may be an upcoming issue. We are the hands of the Lord and some of his best work is done with us helping ourselves, by the ways we use the wisdom that he gives us.

It pleases him to know that he has a great family of his sons and daughters on earth that can build within the kingdom process as he has his faith in us being able to be the brother's keeper he wishes us to become in more ways than one.

Now

To make it clear, this information on how to understand this and how to create peace is in this book.

Now it is about timing because we must put the Lord's plan for prevention in order the way he wants it done to fix something that is broken in America and stop the people from breaking something else by using the wisdom and understanding that the Lord has blessed us with this plan, nothing more or less.

What I Have Done Lately As My Brother's Keeper
(using these books that I have already written and published)

A Peace Offering for the Police and for the People

Distributed press releases all over the USA; gave books away free on Amazon.com and in printed format; had a kiosk billboard located just outside the justice center in Cleveland Ohio for 6 weeks. All promotional expenses have been out of pocket. Featured in interview on 710AM radio in New York City.

Why Do Black Men Harm Each Other More Than Others?

Stopping black on black harm: promoted positive information in the community; voiced aspects of my ministry in open air formats, including but not limited to various local radio station outlets; issues involving police and people; attended various rallies; gave away free copies of books online at Amazon.com; visited local businesses and organizations promoting and selling the book; did a live radio show with the police.

Disconnection of Extremism

To help stop the recruitment of radicalism, extremism, and terrorism; also to help those who have already been radicalized; a campaign for a free give away of book on Amazon.com.

The Unwounding of the U.S. Service Men and Women

Service men and women in America are largest committers of suicide; gave away free books both in print and online at Amazon.com. We need to start a process to help decrease the number of military suicides.

Fixing What is Broken in America By Stopping Towerism

Ran a campaign for days leading up to primary elections in Ohio and five other states, during that time books for free online at Amazon.com; passed out flyers all over the city of Cleveland; sent emails/tweets, etc. attaching flyer throughout country to various media outlets as well as democratic and republican election headquarters. The voting of not the one with towerism – stop towerism – the outcome helps stop the problems in many ways people are having in life!

Read and judge for yourself to be able to help head off a possible national dilemma. This can be looked at is a precursor to a way to end a growth process to understand how to outgrow a part of life that keeps growing on a dark side in an unseen way and thoughts about it is still there.

A ghostly presence of a spirit in America came about because of hatred and bigotry that took place in the 50's and 60's. We witnessed this as black people who were being subjected to brutality. Some white people showed outward hate toward other nationalities also. Now it is displayed in a different kind of war zone that has shown up on a spiritual level more so than the physical one as in the past but now it is somewhat reflected to all people that have the opposite opinion. That is today's dilemma that we all can repair by working together as one with one spirit.

Mankind saw and knew what he was doing before but he cannot see nor does he know all the time what he is doing now. One state of violence was physical; the other is an unseen internal spiritual presence. To add a combination of understanding, what we are developing is preventive measures for stopping spiritual warfare of some unknown presence that can attach to and within the people of America as have been done to others in the world. That is why three books were developed (*Fixing What is Broken in America...*, *The Disconnection of Extremism*, *The Recovery of U.S. Government...*), to help end this issue. This fourth book is developed in conjunction with the other three to stop spiritual warfare in America. It is titled, *Ending Spiritual Warfare in America*. Assistance to all of these books can be accomplished with the help you will be able to receive from the *All Peoples Handbook*, to enhance your spiritual skills. Please read and judge them all for yourself. We may be able to head off a national dilemma.

To further understand the problems within the ungodly system, we are going to reflect back for a minute.

The Exposing

The fact that there are two different kinds of hatred in this world is somewhat unknown or at least not talked about. One is the kind that people have for one another, some more so than others.

It is somewhat a release valve that has an untold amount of respect in it and the other has a pure evil that creates a sickness in their spirit that opens them up to Satan's power that fools them into thinking they are right about what they do and it is not so. At the same time they are like a possessed person.

Now let's try to examine these facts. In the 50's and 60's the people who lived in the south that killed and hung black people had a hatred that was possessed. In the year of 2009 the first black president was placed in office. The hate was there also but it was not like before because there was respect.

Now going back to the 50's and 60's: what made the black people not go to the extreme as whites. One thing was the spiritual will of the living God they possessed and the whites didn't have it on that level. Not saying it's all about all of them because some did who wouldn't participate in the harming of another human, because of knowing the love factor.

Bringing to current years, what has changed? Not much in the hate department accept it has went into darkness and back out of sight until it's time to rear up to make trouble on a large scale. What do I mean? If the people who didn't want the new president in office two times but wouldn't start a war riot, it was because of the goodness of the spiritual power that was in the presence of the people and within the people that Satan could not penetrate.

But when the people gather, and the power of the spirit of love is not there, the power of darkness can open the fury of hell and the vengeance of the devil that he has for the Lord and all of the humans he can captivate to do his will, will prevail.

Now looking at what will be going on at the upcoming convention in Cleveland, Ohio, there will be a 50/50 chance I feel that it may not be enough of the power of love to contain the spirit of darkness and keep it in check. That is why the calling is out to bring the earthly saints and disciples to the forefront to fight off the weakness of mankind because we

We can and must detect, detest and deter any violence and distance ourselves away from it and point it out to let others know we are not a part of the way the prince of darkness wants us to be a part of.

We have the victory in the sight of the Lord and we will be foolish to give it up and let ourselves and the Lord down so we will not see this promise fulfilled. The next steps needed after this convention is over we can look at our lifestyle in the city as a people who broke out of the demonic process where we once were. Now we are free to know we make our own blessings come to past, then the added presence of the wise who will be left that the Lord allows to use the power to see the danger that sometimes mankind has fallen under, that prevents the problem of upcoming trouble on one or more levels.

Then the change of attitudes of live and let live and the key to self-preservation for all people's seeds that will be planted for eternity and forever. Need I say more? Bro. Bush – because actions speak louder than words and show beats tell.

Let Them Keep Their Plans to Themselves

We don't need to know what they are doing and maybe the Lord wants it that way. We have our security with the Lord, because the plans the Lord has for us to see are being revealed. Now how many want to see that plan and also help to carry it out? I will say it like this the heck with what I can't do a thing about and further not to sound too obnoxious. But the part they are doing in protecting the people and city is their job and most people just want to either get in the way and don't know it or are too lazy to do anything to help any way so they want to hear something to make them feel good.

If this be you stop it and really do something if it is only praying; thank you.

How unclear are the facts about this it depended on what side you are on because when people don't see them in the wrong and it can blind them unless they have an open mind and heart.

The facts are clear that if anyone has become radicalized fighting for a faction that is committed to killing others even the innocent, who may have already lost in the battle of self with spiritual warfare.

Ending Spiritual Warfare in America

Insight to be learned that will help keep all people safe

For anyone who needs to understand how to not get involved in a dilemma of principals that are developed on the dark side of reality that can get you trapped and caught up in a function of fiction. It may not seem real at the time but it can cause deadly harm to anyone who falls prey to it. Learn to not fight in wars that we have already won. This book addresses unseen wars. The wisdom it supplies gives a better understanding for a multitude of people and improves their lives while helping to keep them out of danger.

One of the major points that are emphasized is the development of the process that is taking place to elect a new president. There is such a gray area within this process that has not occurred since 1952. Even more so, there can be a new development of positive growth that can come out of this dilemma that the country finds itself in. All parties can benefit from this information and prevent a spiritual war from taking place because of the division that the election process is going through.

The blind spots that have been presented to the people that allowed a negative presence to take control of a certain pattern of growth can be extinguished. The process of ending the miscalculation of candidates running for the office of president of the U.S.A., can create a spiritual warfare which can be prevented.

There are a few chapters that came from the part or the phase I of the new book I hope you will read to get a complete understanding of this new presence of growth pattern.

Next Phase to Enhance Safety

What are some of our suggestions? First, don't worry it is a sin. We don't need doubt in our camp either it is a weakness. Then after learning the truth, we can post up in signs from inside of us to show the future is still bright in the city and the people are safe. So we stop the fear also at the root of what causes it, being blind and not knowing the truth, trusting in the power of the Lord to do what he says he will do.

Now if we see or run into a wrong doing we tell the authorities to stop and apprehend them. This even add extra eyes in the back of the head with bunny rabbit ears. The all peoples handbook may be of help also. What can it help do? Look into all kinds of blind spots that mankind can't. It can be like a development of an extra sensory perception.

Excerpts from "*All Peoples Handbook*"

PHASE 2

Do we understand what the presence of having eyes in the back of heads really stands for or means? If not, it is the extra sensory perception or the combination of the extended special conduit that can receive the power to develop the right equation in a dark place to bring in the light of wisdom, and project it to others in a way that can turn them down if they fill turned up.

It is the yen and yang in you that brings together the spiritual light out of a kind of darkness that is naked to the human eye. That makes a life force that automatically protects life substance out of the element of love. The stronger the love of the Lord that you have in you, the stronger the spiritual skills you deliver to his people.

What can I say? It is somewhat like climbing out of a tunnel in the middle of it using the Son of God that the Lord supplies to bring you to the light of a truth you need. It is also like having a group of angels doing the thinking for you and at the same time, using you to act out the actions and reactions you need to in order to make a safe haven at a time there may be a kind of conflict that needs intervention to create resolve, in spite of the darkness that would like to present itself.

This may occur in a dream or a vision that someone has that can be shared with the authorities to stop and or apprehend the culprit. It all may sound kind of far out there, but if it works on any level, even if it scares off a person who has the idea of doing harm, it's all good.

Just A Thought

Not saying this in a bad way but if you think our commander in chief didn't do a good job and you let someone in that has towerism you are in for a rude awakening and you don't have to take my word for it but I pray it never comes to pass or to our future America first. To get past the place that stops the inner therapy that helps to create change in someone.

At Bound to Heaven Publishing/Ministries we are committed to spiritual guidelines to help see the way out of darkness to free anyone and everyone from bondage of all kinds. This is in the books that are available to be used to help.

This has been a partial summary of what you can learn in the books. First things first: we must stop the worrying and stop the panicking in order to not build up a frenzy with the public's help that enhances the atmosphere where the presence of spiritual begins. That is how Satan works, through panic and frenzy among the people. Therefore, we must not fuel the fire, because the misplacement of this sickness of the people will feed on negativity. We must know that the will of the Lord is in charge.

Now what adds to the downfall is the adults who are too grown to let themselves be taken care of and fixed by the spirit of the Lord within, because they want mankind to fix things and things can't be fixed until they are broken. At the same time, mankind breaks it and or plans to before it can be fixed and that is a kind of sickness that is done in a spirit of darkness.

Therefore, can anyone see this light the Lord is presenting? Can we accept it without trying to figure a way out of the truth? Now if the ounce of prevention worked before our prayers can make them work again. For the unbeliever will you at least not add fuel to the flames for Satan? If you can think on a new level imagine a passport from the evil that wants to fall upon the cities of the USA and how people should pray for the acceptance of peace, by denying admittance.

To Help Starting Today

Now the preventive measures that the governing body of law enforcement has put in place may be a good thing but it is only mankind doing and thinking at work. Let's also take and put the Lord's message of redemption in place to stop and prevent the evil that some people can do from acting out or foolish. We can't ask for more than that from ourselves or anyone else with the Lord on our side.

No brag just a fact: who needs a key to the city when the key to the kingdom of God is at hand to use to help make new cities?

There are a set of values that we must adhere to by being aware of but never atoned for. The values don't come from the principals that Satan has placed in the general areas of life that you define as a place which you should not tread on or in where snakes lie in wait to harm you or destroy you.

There is a warning process and you have been made aware of it regarding the atmosphere which Satan has a certain dominion over upon the planet earth. You cannot deny this fact or escape this reality. You need to be aware of the presence of danger to avoid harm and/or death.

In conclusion, do not be the one who is blind leading the blind or vice-versa.

If you don't hear yourself telling you to open up and let the wisdom in, then you may need to be the one who hits yourself over the head before Satan burns the crap out of you. It is a nasty but real truth.

Public Notice

The announcement has gone out that Satan is having a party but from this day forward, the plan for this gathering has been cancelled, by order of the Holy Spirit that was voted on in heaven with the approval of the Godly minded saints on earth. The invitation has been abolished and the decree for this was announced on Resurrection Day of our Lord and Savior 2016.

Once again the rift that Satan wants to bring forth has been put out of the cities on earth due to the fact that it is no longer wanted or needed to settle the people's problem to raise up some kind of hell on earth or to make a point that can be made in a peace filled way.

The tricks of long ago have gone sour and new seed has been sown upon the earth within the people. It can't be removed or taken away. It can make sure that by the people starting to work in the will of the father in this way, we don't lose our place as a people in the body of Christ, when the time comes to increase the number that will be going to heaven before of the rapture taking its course in history.

This Play is Titled;
A Cancellation of Satan's Party at the 2016 RNC

We are hereby decreasing the bypassing of the way the earthly beast of the atmosphere has led some of the people in the past. We are now presenting a halo of peace to be worn by the people to give them the power to fix and settle many ways of conflict without violence; In the name of Jesus in the presence of the Holy Spirit.

There Will Not be Any Witches
Stew or Warlock Brew Served

The violence has invited itself to see how prone we can be of ourselves, as it was in the City of Cleveland, Ohio at a time when other cities were getting torn apart and down. This we do in agreement with knowing a better day can come to the lives of many for the act of peace we are showing the world that they may not know what has taken place in the city what gave us a pathway to show we can repent from our sins by stopping the evil doing with the power the Lord has given us to use wisely, as he wishes.

May the peace be with us as we wear our halo proudly.
Amen and hallelujah

Now we can wear our halos to show we have purchased our way as actors in this real life performance. The play will be played out in real life.

Now can we have everyone receive a ticket to this real life enactment that is unfolding to and in front of mankind? This is the last phase of the play that is in writing for mankind to live within a part of it. The first act of kindness that the Lord showed us is already up online in its book form to be received.

What may be the great part about what is taking place in the city of Cleveland, Ohio? The wisdom to cancel the party planner plans for his next one and the next one he wants to have can be cancelled also, using the same techniques once you find out he has a plan for one, start the process of planting seeds of love to outgrow the wicked spirit that wants to take root and cause an ungodly spell on the unprotected and somewhat innocent to draw them in because they have no armor of the Lord that they are wearing.

Therefore, the traps are placed with a covering of God's love and a crown of a halo to give them the insight along with the fact they have studied this law of the living God as it was sent forth to be placed in the hearts of mankind.

Give thanks to the Lord for all of our victories in the presence of his will being done.

Act II

This is the beginning of the ending of a large part of Satan's madness. The invitation was put out by the Clump and what I consider one of the most harmful and hateful things anyone can do is invite the devil to be a part of a party.

That is why this notice has been sent out to lead the demons of darkness that carry around the skulls and crossbones that are lost from a negative pathway to a heavenly state of mind. The party that was planned is no longer going to be held and therefore the services of the hosts of the ghosts of the dead and if there are some who are of the walking dead they too are not needed, that includes, the butcher, the baker and candlestick maker.

The prince of darkness has been given notice to go back to hell and stay there at this time of the upcoming RNC party and all of his followers may join him if they haven't figured out it is a hoax and who needs a death wish, just to be seen, as a demon in a small part to play in life, because there are greater parts that cost less than what some have given their time and energy to take on that creates a peace of mind with the power of true love that backs them up off of the high and byways of darkness; then puts them on a level of having clouds in the sky on a natural high that money can't buy.

Therefore, the changing of the guard in the way we need to live has come to the present and it is up to all people no matter what race, creed or color you are to give in to a kindling spirit that will show you the way out of madness, sadness to a place of gladness with happiness to be shared among everyone in all of the days to follow.

Weather the weather because it in time will make you clever and wise. A part of Act II - now get the first book to clear the gray to make the blue shine through.

What does it stand for? A good time to be had and for the people to prosper not to see their labor taken away in vain and destroyed, thanks to the foresight of the Lord to put a plan in place shows he is still in control of life, especially the part that leads to ever after.

The Play

How many people would rather receive their reward in heaven than on earth? It seems like not many who may not really believe in heaven.

Hear Ye, Here Ye

Read all about it to a true life dream that comes to an end for the party pooper that breaks up the party and causes some kind of hell as it does it.

It is time to see an unfolding of a play of great proportion unfold right before your eyes. An era of time has come to unveil the truth of what has caused so many problems in the past and have not been stopped because of not knowing a way. At this time, there is a way to stop the hell raising read about it to see how it unfolds right before your eyes. Get the book to help stop the crook that can no longer bust up a party.

This play has many participant including the writer. His major role is preaching love anointing yearning. The audience is to sit in witness wisdom to the power of the pen who the Lord lays hand on a hand of a man or a child of his. Therefore, for the millions of people who don't believe enjoy it is time to grow some new phase of faith in your life. The calling is within your ears if you have a mind to listen.

You may take this as a warning or a wake-up call. Satan has raised the bar on his worker he has them building new kiln to house the fires he has going. But the unconsidered part of this is in the making of them he has adapted an old hateful system that was put on the slaves of Israel by the people of Egypt. It is for them to make the bricks without the needed straw and he is trying to up the tally.

Therefore, if he is doing this to the workers who are already in his kingdom of hell how much more do you think he is doing to win your vote? This is the play; read it; study it then live your part in it. The Lord will love you for it.

Back to your part: all it requires is for you to study the scriptures the Lord has set up for you. Then stay out of the way of one another. Do no more or less and let the evens play out. The guidelines are simple and a way to foul the process up is letting your emotions get in your way and then stepping out of line on someone else's toes as the it factor wants you to do to get trouble started and then the play has or will have a missed que in it and the people will get the lines wrong.

This can mean a not so good ending. Therefore, if you don't know your mind, you don't know your lines. Therefore, know your mind to stop from creating a problem that may be the issues that cause harm to others. It is so very important to know if you can't say anything nice at a party, don't say are our brother's keepers. The process of this kind of wisdom blocks and stops the phase of the unknown spiritual warfare that Satan can use as he has before, to creep in to take the unprotected into his army to make them his slaves and commit sins against other people.

When we understand what these principals of the power of Satan have, we strip him of his ability to use us as humans and put us under his bondage and take us on a journey that we can't control and it could even send us to hell.

That is why the freedom bells must ring out throughout the city at a time with many churches together to let Satan know we are on watch. It is a time for a calling to become watchmen.

I ask you will the bells be a sign of the cross over? Will the good of mankind prevail over evil that wants to inflict a kind of hell on the inhabitants and dwellings the people use? It would like to but it can't thanks again to no weapons formed against us shall prosper in Jesus name. We must work together to put God's miracles in order; not only cover ourselves with what mankind who live in darkness and fear of a new way to change does not want us to know of and about.

This is a declaration that has been proposed by the laws of the land as a spiritual law to life. In order to complete the concept of project peace, we must believe, think and know that the atmosphere has changed.

There must be a discerning of us as a people from the plagues that want to fall upon us in order for it to affect the city.

anything at all, because we know the one it factor that is guaranteed to not forget their line and that is Satan. He is lying in wait for anyone to missed ques in order for him to pounce up and land on to get his party started the way it is best at. That is making trouble for the people who may not see it coming and for those who expect it because of their blindness to know that it is a way out of the chaos and mayhem in life and the Lord provides a way and even a blind man can see that once they become worded up with the wisdom of the Lord.

Therefore, be ye not blind or deaf and let yourself become wise in order to not let the darkness become the light that gives no truth sight to your eyes in the place of trouble that hides out in people's minds until it can reveal itself.

Know your mind and renew your heart so you can take part in the real party to come at the end of this life. Let's keep it 100 and get down to our father's business as he wishes and not like Satan wants us to.

There are two parts to this real life reenactment. The one played by humans the other played by Satan. Now humans have faults and are somewhat lazy at times. That is a problem and it should be corrected now because Satan is not. It is one of the most skillful things that ever presented it is an earthly and on time creature of an unseen force.

It has no time to waste in taking as many victims as it can. Therefore, if you get one step behind the move it wants to take in the process of thinking you just might be out thought by it/him or whatever you name it. Don't lose your thoughts because it is more cunning than you ever need to find out.

This real life reenactment is over the way you came in is the way you can leave out of the process of growth. Know this is an beginning to an end of the problem that Satan tries to create for the people of the world. News: spread the good news that the gospel of the Lord is also renewing the spirit of mankind still in mighty ways and this is just one way to let his truth be revealed and it is nice to know how well this play has gone because the whole process to and was a gift from the Lord.

Play no part for Satan at the party. You are exiled from be able to steal my joy away from me. For all things work together for the good of those who love the Lord and shall prosper. The saints are few but steady. It is time to get out of the void-noid sin-drome.

The Big Deal
Big Ticket

This is the plan the Lord has put in place in order to keep the order with the people in the land.

There are two phases: the first will come last. It has already been put out on Amazon.com in a book titled, *Ending Spiritual Warfare in America*. The second is in the development state of a drama process of what we can look at as if it is a play.

To Repeat

To the people of Cleveland, Ohio: we have good news. You wanted answers to what is going to be done to protect and prevent the city and people from harm and damage. Well, it is not a one way process and the plan that has been put in place by the government and law enforcement are not to be revealed completely but the plan the Lord has for the way he will protect the city and people has been revealed.

This is it: Hello from the governing body of the presence of the Lord that is presenting healthy hearts, healthy minds and healthy souls that create a healthy spirit.

Phase I Make it clear

We can put together enough volunteers to help with getting the word out about what is going on with the country it is OK to make know a part of life that may be in danger from letting the duck get close to the White House

This has been put together a plan to save the city and people from harm with phase1 that can also help the people who live in the USA to show The road to lead the people out of the danger who are lost from the truth in the byways and highways of the country – on all levels, even though they don't believe in what we are doing at BTHPM.

I am dividing to conquer the problems we may be facing with the right ideas that can change the outcome of what appears to be a bleak future, bleak outlook on tomorrow's forecast.

Please Listen Up

Even if you are one of the people who cannot truly help support this cause, we can win with the love we have in our hearts.

I do have a problem when it comes down to how I can make the proper introduction with the conveyance of information, because we can end the risk of losing a part of the growth we have going on in Cleveland, Ohio.

It is my hope that there will be given enough of a scenario to draw a conclusion from. In act II of the living play. That is meant to stop the problem of people being overly concerned about the problems the city of Cleveland, Ohio may face it and about the upcoming convention.

There has been put together a solution to clear up or clean up the troubles that could have or may have arisen. It is now up to the people to imbed it upon themselves in a way or ways to believe it can happen but foremost it must start from the heart and work its way up to their mind sight to see the possible.

Do you have an idea how it feels to have a gift that can see something that others wish they could? I hope so.

I must admit its existence to be able to unfold a mystery that the hands of time has held or is holding on to that will come to pass in the right way because providence has had its place to show its way that it has been into that includes a human effort.

There is so much to be covered in life at times it seems like you may not know how or where to start in. So I will jump in by saying congratulations to whomever it may concern.

Now what may be the biggest problem with this not coming to pass in the right way? It is people not trusting what God said. The people have had so many things broken in their lives and around their lives they feel that it is a given, to the people and by the people to break something at a certain time and place. But this can be changed. If you believe now more so than ever, if people can go to and support the other venues in the city of Cleveland then why not give this a chance. It may make Cleveland believerland and cleverland, the next great hope land.

Therefore, let's try something on a greater level than we may have had no idea could give us more growth in the city. But foremost let's trust the Lord together without the separation of state.

Lift the Scales

The people that have been branded its only because of one reason, they did it themselves Satan can't brand anyone, but he will make you think he has or can. 999 is the level of life we can shoot for in our thinking and it was the period of time old man methuselah lived.

Become One Who is Noble

Inside the script there are the blue prints to a detail used by Satan but we have the outline to conquer the unseen enemy to stop him.

This is a part of a makeover wish from prayers that have been answered to end a dimension of the wolf pack mob mentality.

M-N

The Lord has applied his own kind of medication that clears the vision and excites the emotional sense of whoever needed a renewal from before that they may have been a dead person walking.

Together we can will the enemy to pass by the City of Cleveland, Ohio and the people of Philadelphia, PA, can do the same. We can all keep the love growing. This is our way to be a part of the possible.

The Bright People

The bright people will always keep in mind that they should never let Satan creep or sneak up on them to spend time with them. It will be a bad influence on them what it suggests.

Therefore, don't get caught sleeping on your two feet. Be aware of your surroundings even when you are supposed to be awake.

A Bridge

The hardest bridge to complete is a bridge that requires no stone, no mortar, no steel. The bridge that I am talking about is the bridge of acceptance. There are so many things that people have problems with accepting. It is an endless battle that has harmed more humans than possibly all the wars in all the nations in the lands on earth.

People cannot accept the truth of this because our sin nature has branded lots of people from what they saw, heard and experienced. The key to ending the past parts of life that created devastation that wounded so many humans is the rebirth of a spiritual awakening. That can be one of the most monumental moments that change the course of history in someone's life. We get to that moment by accepting the thin gs that we sometimes do not understand. The things that are without a presence of reality but can only be touched through the spirit.

If you are old enough to read this and have a slight indication of how to comprehend what is being explained to you, then your ability to examine facts leads you to bring about thoughts that will be read and have been written before you read them. This means one thing, there has to be some kind of pain that is included in your gain. There has to be a loss column in order to bring about a win column. What do you have that has caused you to lose more than you should.

Now you can determine the outcome of your ability to do one thing that I hope you are already doing, thinking for yourself. This is the premises of the writing that you have read to give you a better understanding of how you can do this with the least amount of complication possible. This will create the greatest amount of success.

The Turmoil of Un-Stroking of the Ego

Stroking the ego is a hard thing to deal with. It is like loving someone and they don't appreciate your love. At the same time you can't stop until the blues hit the fan and the funk makes a mud-hole and you keep stepping in when you think about it, until you give in or give up and take a trip to one place. It is one of the hardest places for anyone to go and that is the heart-break hotel.

Now, who knows once you go there how long people will have to stay and that is one reason lots of people are afraid of that place even more so than some are afraid of death. That is so wrong and this is also a part of the spiritual warfare that some people get trapped into. They really don't want to be there but the reality has gotten so distorted they think of it as maybe some kind of paradise that comes after death. How wrong they could be; no, how wrong they are!

Getting back to the point: for some people, accepting what has been written could be like stepping into a heart break hotel that creates fear of being alone and unhappy. But, if you have an ounce of hope in you, it can turn into happiness in time and if you lose the fear factor you outgrow yourself.

Right now in the presence of the spirit man with in you, bring the joy out of a dark place to know it is love that conquers all. You don't ever have to face the fear factors alone, even if it may seem like it, because it is an illusion of Satan that doesn't want you to get on the other side of the bridge where heaven may be waiting for you.

If I had the help to navigate my way out of the spiritual warfare, the least I can do is show others how to cause the devil to pass them by – on a bypass that can be found on the highways and sky-ways of the spiritual workings in the world. It is nowhere near all bad. Now don't make up the plan people!

This plan also draws a new level of people to its presence. These people admire the new sight and presence of a thing of beauty, even though it will never be touched by human hands. But does this really matter? It depends on who you are. I said it as if the angels can do something the people on earth would do if they could, but can't, unless they get a halo and wings in a place in time.

The new frame of reality now is coming into focus. It leads us to believe that those individuals who have kept so many people in fear of their power that they possess, are falling from grace. This was a manmade camouflage of grace that was used to intimidate, antagonize and control others with their arrogance and egotistic reality that they presented in an unethical manner. Now it has an unveiling that can be seen and identified. Therefore, the evidence we hold truth to and witness to, such as the latest towers that are falling – part of the Panama papers that people have been subject to discrimination, demoralization and all other negative consequences that was projected toward those who were considered peasants by those in towers.

Now, as God is no respecter persons and we can see a new day where all men are created equal. Every man should feel as if he is equal to the best of men and inferior to none. This gives the freedom of not fearing the opposition as David did with Goliath.

Silence is Golden

The division is to not make the enemy that is of negativity, aware of the plan by putting it right in front of them because they are so negative that they may think it is not going to work in the first place as was when they almost got trumped!

Now the question I have left is: can this process turn some of the thinking that people have around? Is it time to know of a new visceral way of viewing things?

Note

For some this may become one of the first intimate chances to gain a better way to view life, by way of this spiritual journey. Enjoy it and the freedom that comes with it because the more the people of earth go there, the better off the planet's balance becomes because it is an intimacy wherein you receive a divine intervention.

As For Me and the Division of My Blood Line

There was a time (I learned at puberty) when I, as a descendent of native people, knew how to fight a spiritual warfare. This may be one of the reasons I can because I have performed a spiritual war dance to bring about peace between people who were black and white.

The time has come to unify the harmony. It can be the music of light that song cannot beat.

Welcome to a state of using common sense to become a spiritual activist.

People like me who need people: are you the luckiest people in the world?

It is time for people who had no business there to be recruited from the spiritual war zone – it is a place to tell yourself, if you are feeling disappointed about life, you are not a part of it within yourself because you are a child of the most high and he loves you. Satan wants you to harm your physical being and make you think your spiritual being will be alright but this isn't true. It is the final straw that takes you out of and away from the Lord's kingdom.

It is not fair to oneself or anyone else to walk around with the chip on your shoulder that could insight a spiritual warrior, who has no idea what they are doing in a battle with self at times and wanting to share it with others. The pathway has been made clear.

There are no strings attached to the crossover being that wants to take you there in the fight no matter what kind of fight or who it is with; it can stop. The enemy's plan has been told and it doesn't take a rocket scientist to break it down to stop from acting like a foolish cluck. Wise up and take charge because you have been made to be more than a conqueror and stop letting Satan con you.

To understand another kind of truth: it was not easy for me to get the chip off of my shoulder of the presence of me in the war zone. But my family helped me do it and they didn't know what they were doing lots of times. I feel some even wanted to go to the next world to help me and I don't doubt that fact.

Stop

This may be a shorter hop to help you move away from negativity in order to keep you moving on to a better way to think and live.

This knowledge may be a key to the power brought forth to help mankind step down to a better way of life because everything doesn't have to be a step up.

To Not Sound Sarcastic

There has been a problem with people who have been spiritually dormant for centuries. The problem of spirituality needs to be unlocked or renewed in order for them to be able to see the new level of presence. We can use this as a people to deny any kind of unethical and immoral system that may be put in place already or attempted to be put in place.

The fact of the matter is, we cannot trust each other in a present state of being that we rely on totally to make things right for us in the governing system that we exist under, unless we create a total referendum to examine the policies and facts that people want us to live under by the jurisdiction of the laws given to them.

We must develop a new set of justice that creates a level of elimination of injustice that has caused an impartial development of growth in our society. I do not ever want to seem as if I am making statements on a philosophical basis but the reality remains we must constantly correct and improve the system and standards that we live under and by.

Therefore, find your proper place to be within the body of Christ and do not settle for anything less in order for you to give the best you can to the life you live.

If you disagree with anything you have read, you can feel free to re-write it in your own perspective. But whatever you do, don't ignore the main point: love can be developed on every side of life where there is a challenge, but evil must be eliminated.

This is a new process of learning that starts off with a healthcare plan that prepares the digestive system to receive the proper food and nutrition. This spiritual and soul food has been prepared to not reject or regurgitate it because of the system not being able to handle it. The meal has been prepared from this stage with love: now enjoy it!

What is the Biggest Trick Satan Places in the Spiritual War Zone?

It is the craziest part about all of this because some people go there in anger and do not know it, and wind up killing someone or dead themselves. It is one of Satan's hooks and that is why the Lord supplies us with Cool-ade to help us stay away from Satan's heat.

What can be said other than Satan jumps in control to do his dirty work. He uses people for this purposes and jumps out of it. People wind up paying for it. This should not be a part of life because it was not meant to be. We can eliminate it and not add it to the life we live.

This all adds up to the elements we seek to free us from the petrified forest that is a gateway that Satan stands guard over to enter hell.

An Answer to People's Concerns and Prayers

The people have made it known that they want answers to what the protectors of the people are going to do to protect the people and the city. They have heard some answers but they still feel they need more.

Now if you can stand the truth how about forgetting about what man can do to protect your interests and find out what the Lord has planned for the protection of the City of Cleveland residents and its visitors. Therefore if your mind and heart is ready to not only know the Lord's plan but to also be a part in the living play as a participant, you can. That is right you are invited to the first of its kind active play that has the script for people to follow written out in a book that will make more than conquerors out of us in stopping the potential problems at the upcoming RNC in Cleveland, Ohio.

The book that delivers the information is titled, _The Devil Passed Me By_. It will give you all the details you can find it at Amazon.com, search Bro. Tracy Bush. This is a few of the other books I have authored and ways I have helped to end the different problems we face in life in society. The Lord will give us a supernatural way to grow if we let him.
.

The goal is to promote as much as possible so that everyone in and around Cleveland, or those who will be visiting, the opportunity to read the book and play their part in keeping our City (and country) a great and safe place to live, and getting better every day.

Thank you for whatever kind of contribution you can give. An account has been set up, www.gofundme.com/nzp42cys, to receive your donation to help get the word out in time, before the upcoming RNC. Here are the details:

- For your immediate contribution, a Certificate will be provided acknowledging your donation;
- Contributions will be used for marketing and advertising, to insure that millions can be able to receive this book for free.
- Giveaway to begin end of April or beginning of June, depending on contributions;
- The book is currently available for purchase in eBook format, on Amazon.com, at a cost of $4.11.

We as a people are our best defense against the foolish, who want to try to harm us and this is a way to break into a supernatural state of creating oversight, to protect the people and the land.

This is a tip of the iceberg of what Bound to Heaven is doing that can help make the world a better place to live. Thank you and may God continue to bless America more than ever. There are other books Bro bush has author online at Amazon.com, all under $5.00.

For more information regarding Bro. Tracy Bush and the books he has written, email tb.bthpm@gmail.com or visit www.boundtoheaven.org.

CERTIFICATE OF ACKNOWLEDGMENT

I, _____, hereby acknowledge the necessity to avoid all traps set by Satan from now through the rest of my life. I will strive to do my part in this living play. In doing so, I recognize that no weapons formed against me shall prosper.

I claim victory over spiritual wars that want to show up through the ungodly ways of violence to tear down and harm people. I will do my part to cancel the party pooper's (b.k.a. Satan) plans with the help of a living play that shows what the power of love can do.

Bound to Heaven Publishing/Ministries
Thanks you for your assistance!

Bro. Tracy E. Bush
CEO, BTHPM
Notes

_____

_____

_____

_____

_____

_____

_____

_____

_____

_____

_____

_____

_____

_____

_____

Philippians 4:17
17. Not that I seek the gift, but I seek the fruit that abounds to your account.

Acts 20:24
24. But none of these things move me; nor do I count my life dear to myself, so that I may finish my race with joy, and the ministry which I received from the Lord Jesus, to testify to the gospel of the grace of God.

www.ingramcontent.com/pod-product-compliance
Lightning Source LLC
Chambersburg PA
CBHW061805280526
45787CB00003BA/1488